The Wine Appreciation Guild
360 Swift Avenue
South San Francisco, CA 94080
(650) 866-3020
www.wineappreciation.com

Design and Illustrations by Roger Roberts
Text by Judy Valon
Pre-Press by C. Worthington

The Authors assert their moral rights to be identified as the Authors of this work.
Library of Congress Control Number: 2006933772

ISBN: 1-891267-93-0
ISBN 13: 978-1-891267-93-2

Printed in China

Vine Lines

A well balanced and humorous exploration of wine terminology

Dedicated to all wine lovers!

This book has been designed to make you laugh, giggle a little and enjoy and appreciate wine even more than you do now!

The Wine Appreciation Guild
San Francisco

Contents

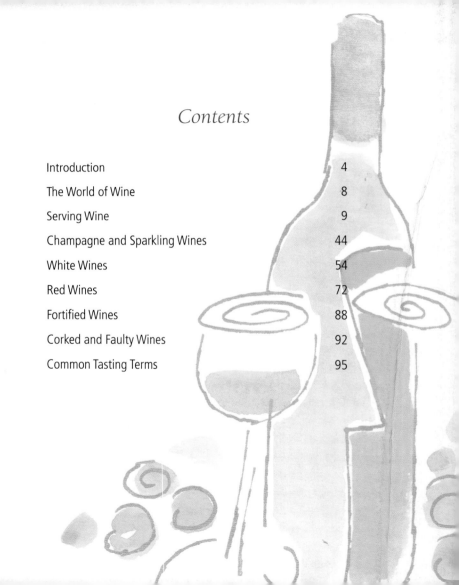

Introduction 4

The World of Wine 8

Serving Wine 9

Champagne and Sparkling Wines 44

White Wines 54

Red Wines 72

Fortified Wines 88

Corked and Faulty Wines 92

Common Tasting Terms 95

Wine is life
PETRONIUS, ROMAN WRITER

Dear Fellow Wine lovers

Flabby, acidic, good nose, well constructed, citrus overtones, a hint of sweaty saddle. These are some of the descriptions out there, what applies to what? Then there is the debate of cork vs screw caps, what constitutes a good wine, how long should it be laid down, what should I drink with what and the list goes on ....

The world has had a fascination with wine for thousands of years. We have become a lot more sophisticated in our tastes over the last 20 years and subsequently have increased our consumption quite considerably over that time. The "New World" wines are of outstanding quality and bear excellent comparison with the more established traditional markets, with their success now clearly evident on the global scene.

Wine forms part of our every day lives, we drink to accompany fine and exotic foods, we drink to celebrate, to alleviate a hard stressful day at work and sometimes we drink just because we want to and because we can! Whoever you are, whatever the occasion, wherever you are, there is a wine style perfectly suited.

Wine appeals to our senses, sight, smell and taste. From the design of the label to the colour of the wine and shape of the bottle, we are seduced. The popping of a champagne cork being pulled or the more subtle sigh of a wine cork and the first splash of wine poured into the glass, the first swill releasing the wonderful aromas, all attack our senses with anticipation and desire.

Traditionally wines are chosen to match with food; however, you can drink any wine with any style of food.

There are of course elements of wine that will react differently to food, these are essentially, tannin, sugar, acid content and the alcohol level, but it all boils down to a personal choice and taste. Those of you who do food match discerningly will experience unique and stunning taste sensations that others will never experience and therefore will not miss.

Wine provides pleasure and entertainment and gives those avid collectors a reason to spend more money and more time in their cellars. We watch them age lovingly and fantasise about that special occasion when we will get to savour that unique drop. There are of course that breed of true wine connoisseurs (and the would be's), a much rarer breed who tend to be too critical in their prejudices. Wine should be seen as an ingredient to social intercourse and all that is required to fully appreciate it is a reasonable sense of smell and taste and an interest in the extensive varieties available to us.

This book is designed to give you a light and humorous illustrative overview of some of the most commonly used and some of the more obscure terms used to describe wines. "Wine-speak", "wine waffle", call it what you will, it exists and it is used to describe the smell, taste and aftertaste. The terms we have illustrated just may assist you in making more "intelligent" noises when in the company of those wine "connoisseurs".

We want this book to make you laugh and smile and recall the images as you use the terms when tasting or experiencing those first aromas and to derive even more pleasure from wine than you do today!
Cheers!

P.S. Life is too short to drink bad wine

well developed

mellow

The world of wine

*W*ine gives us pleasure, that's the whole point of it! It plays a major role in our social infrastructure, it's an indulgence, mood enhancer and stress reliever and in moderation has some certain health advantages. Red wine has been reported to be full of antioxidants and can be effective in lowering the bad cholesterol which can lead to cardio vascular disease and more recently, discoveries have been found that antioxidants in white wine could be more effective than those in red. To be safe drink both!

From looking outside the industry in, the world of wine appears complicated, it is not. However from the many and varied descriptions that are used you may at first think so!

The varieties available and their descriptions may daunt you but remember there are no rules. Learning more about wine is easy, enjoy the myriad of cellar doors throughout the world, taste and try different wines, experience wines that you might not always drink or want to drink. The good cellar door and indeed liquor store are invaluable to assist us in making a good choice, notice I did not say the right choice, as there is no right or wrong. Start with the basic grape varieties and build your knowledge and experience from there.

Wine regions are some of the most beautiful parts of the world, so get out there and visit them. Wine is steeped in history and has religious symbolism dating back centuries.

Personally I love to enjoy wine with food, it seems odd not to have a glass with a meal, except perhaps with breakfast, but there are those slow weekend breakfasts that cry out for a glass of sparkling – exquisite!

Some basic rules of thumb for serving wine

Pre Lunch / Dinner drinks:
Sherry, Champagne or sparkling wine, lighter style white wines (red wine is better served with food). These are regarded as appetite stimulants and are perfect served with olives, nuts or light nibbles.

During the meal – commence with the lighter style wines to accompany an entrée, whites or a light red, moving through to a heavier bodied wine for the main course.

To serve with dessert you cannot go past a luscious sweet or fortified wine, such as a Spatlese or Botrytis Riesling.

To round off the meal, with perhaps some cheese and for total indulgence there are exquisite fortified wines such as Muscat, Madeira or Port.

Enjoy and Bon Appetit!

Wine makes every meal an occassion, every table more elegant, every day more civilised

ANDRE SIMON

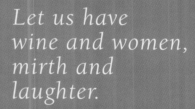

Penicillin cures but wine makes people happy

SIR ALEXANDER FLEMING

Let us have wine and women, mirth and laughter.

Sermons and soda water the day after

LORD BYRON DON JUAN

laying it down

delicate
rose
petal
nose

a heavy red

(At his first sip of champagne) Come quickly I am tasting stars

Dom Perignon

bottle aged

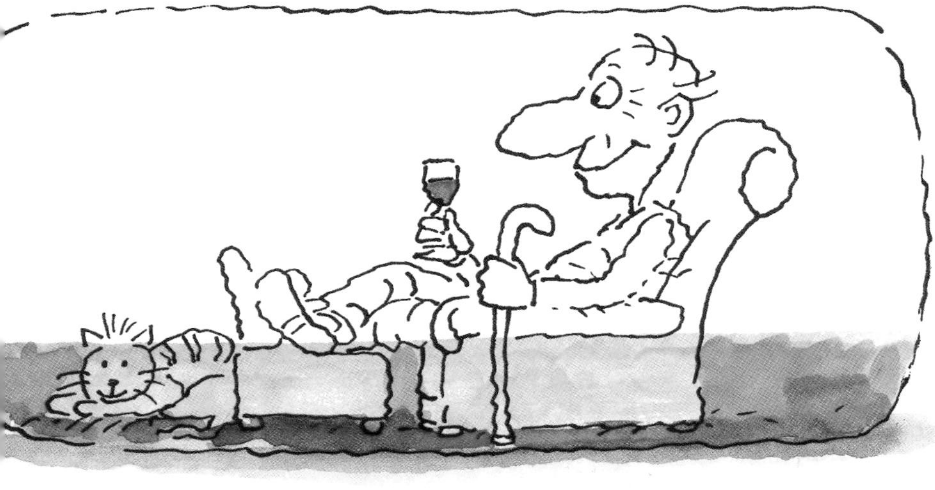

approachable
at a younger age

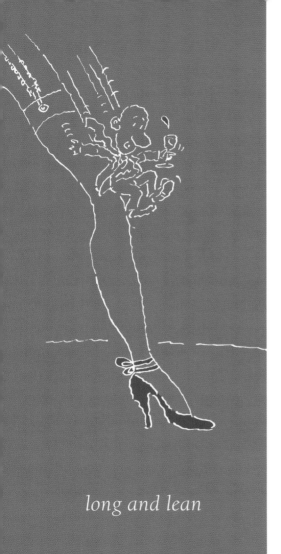

long and lean

She gets to keep the
chalet and the Rolls,
I want the Montrachet

ANONYMOUS, FORBES MAGAZINE,
MAY 6, 1996

Wine.... the intellectual
part of the meal

ALEXANDER DUMAS

Good wine is a necessity
of life for me

THOMAS JEFFERSON

*In victory,
you deserve
Champagne,
in defeat,
you need it*

NAPOLEON BONAPARTE

*If food is the body
of good living,
wine is its soul*

CLIFTON FADIMAN

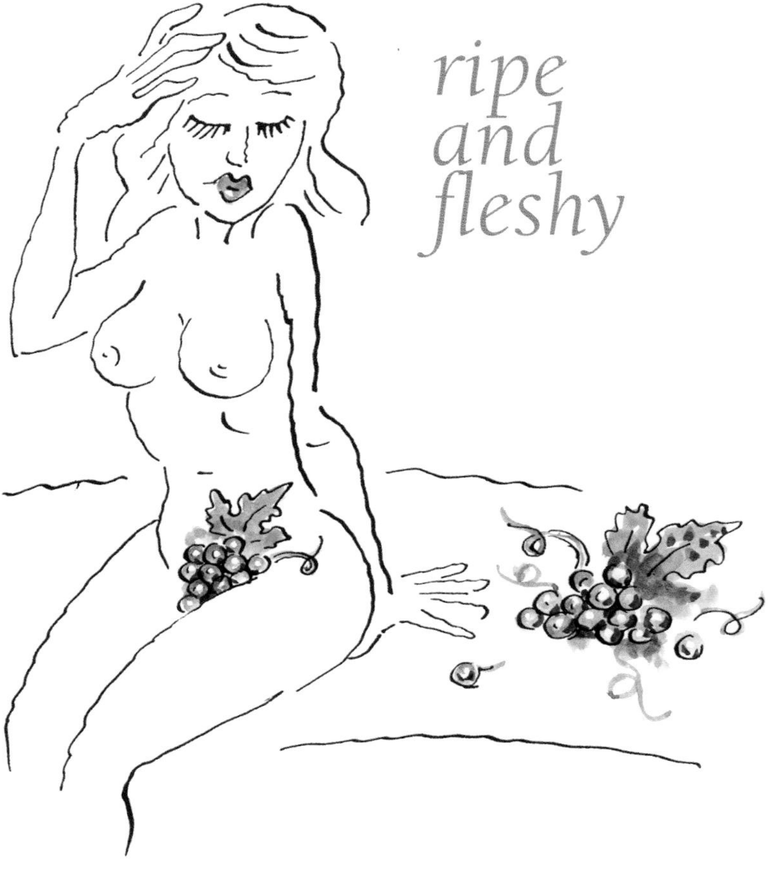

ripe and fleshy

bacon character

horizontal tasting

distinctive nose

powerful

tightly wound

full bodied

When
I read
about the
evils of
drinking,
I gave up
reading

HENNY YOUNGMAN

*long
and
silky*

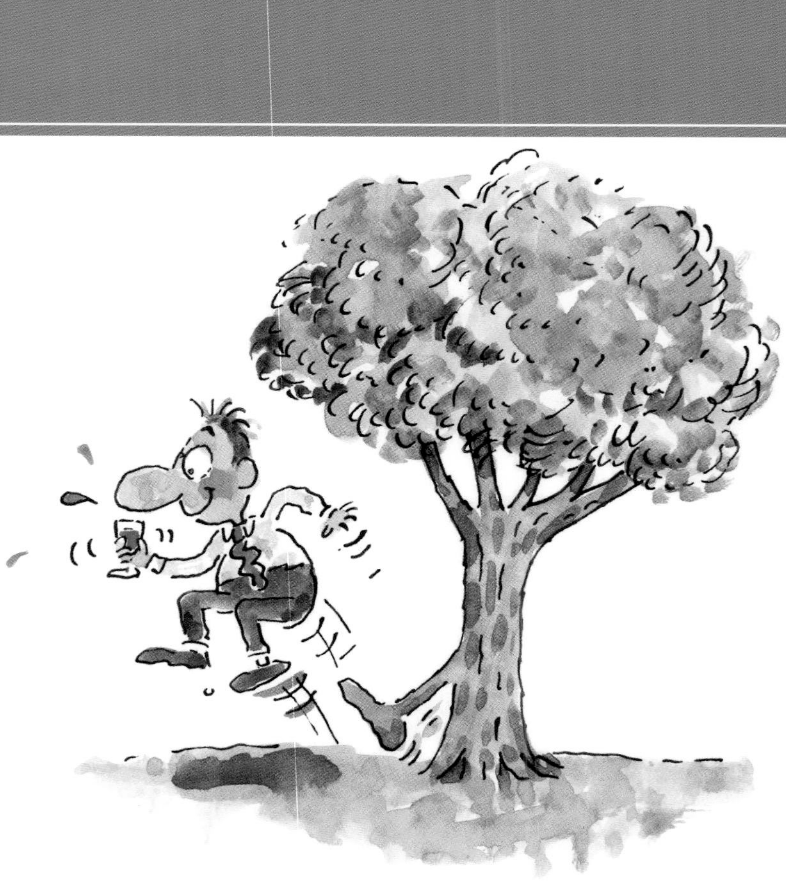

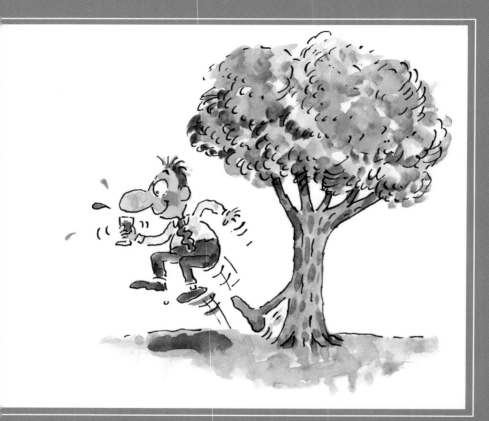

extra kick from the oak

*fleshy
overtones*

lithe and elegant

youthful aromas

shows promise

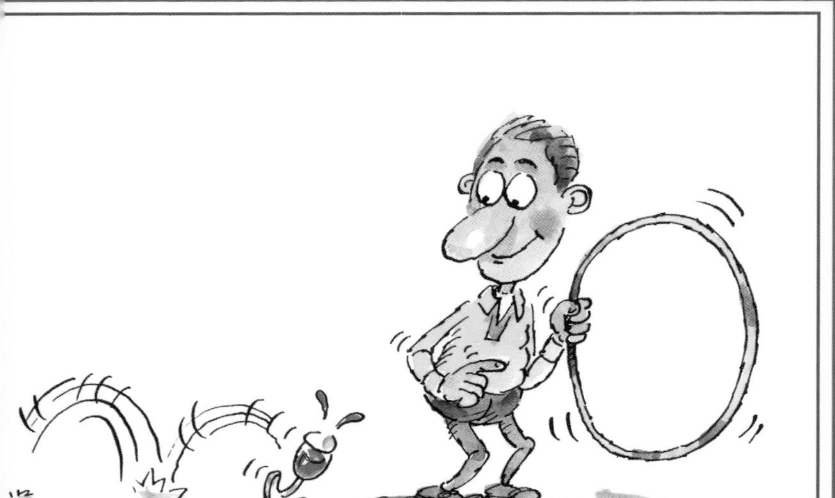

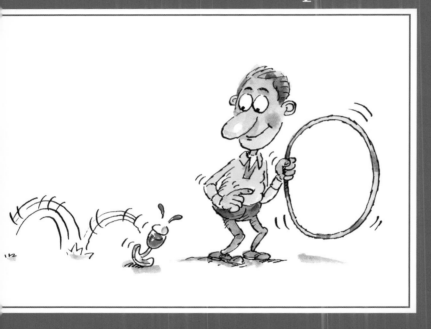

hollow

Men are like wine–some turn to vinegar, but the best improve with age

POPE JOHN XXIII

mature

*There are only two occasions when I drink
Champagne, and these are:
when I have game for dinner and when I haven't*

ATTRIBUTED TO S.D.CHURCHILL

Compromises are for relationships, not wine

SIR ROBERT SCOTT CAYWOOD.

*Wine makes daily living easier, less hurried,
with fewer tensions and more tolerance*

BENJAMIN FRANKLIN

volatile

*Alcohol - the cause of and solution
to all of life's problems*

"Wine is life" I have heard it said
It is drunk most nights before we hit bed
Very good for us in moderation we hear
So we should do our bit and avoid the beer

To celebrate or just have with a meal
Wine is the ultimate drink I feel
We share a glass of bubbles or two
When we get married and say we do

We open a bottle when friends come around
To share a success or some news just found
It helps de-stress, relax and wind down
Or party with friends for a night on the town

JUDY VALON

structured and chewy

extracted palate

light bodied

*high
acidity*

fun
and
frivolous

Champagne and Sparkling Varieties

Champagne, Sparkling, Fizz, Bubbles – whenever a sparkling cork is pulled, there is an uplifting celebratory feeling, whether it is a celebration or special event, served as an aperitif or just because.....!

Methode traditionelle is the method used in Champagne, and is essentially a secondary fermentation inside the bottle where sugar and yeast is added to the wine. This produces further alcohol and creates the wonderful sparkles. The bottles are then aged on lees (sur lie) from 6 months to 3 years, resulting in delightful wine that has wonderful toasty, yeasty and fruit flavours.

The above method is however very labour intensive and takes years to produce a quality product. Currently there are more economical ways that have been developed that can produce a finished wine in months vs years, however they do not provide the interest and character of methode traditionelle.

There is a large range of both white and red sparkling wines, that are kinder to the wallet and allow us to drink regularly, as we should. Bubbles are perfect for breakfast, lunch and dinner and any time in between!

My only regret in life is that I did not drink more Champagne

JOHN MAYNARD KEYNES

barnyard

creamy

*I drink it when I'm happy
and when I'm sad
Sometimes I drink it when I'm alone
When I have company
I consider it obligatory
I trifle with it if I'm not hungry
and I drink it when I am
Otherwise I never touch it,
unless I'm thirsty*

Madame Lily Bollinger

earthy

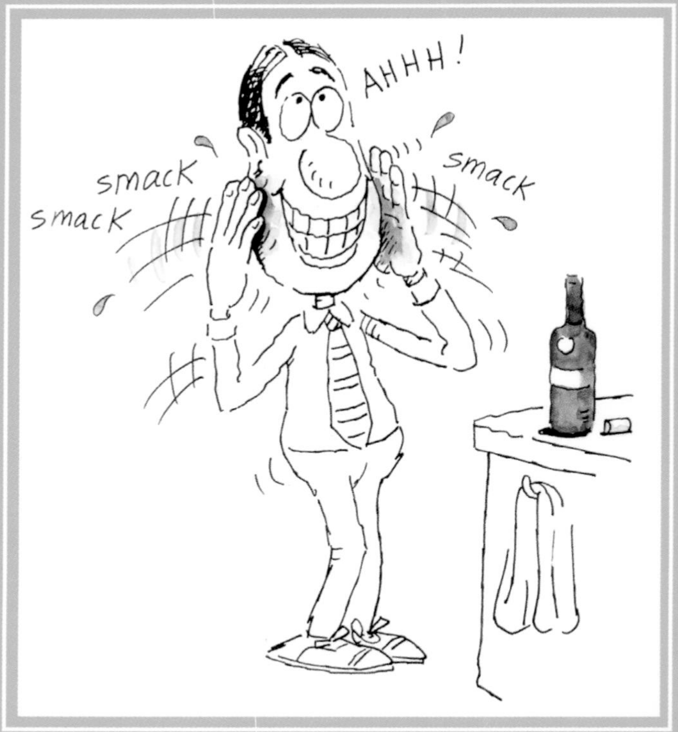
AHHH!
smack
smack
smack

perfumed

chocolate

Burgundy makes you think of silly things,
Bordeaux makes you talk of them
and champagne makes you do them

JEAN-ANTHELME BRILLAT-SAVARIN

truffle

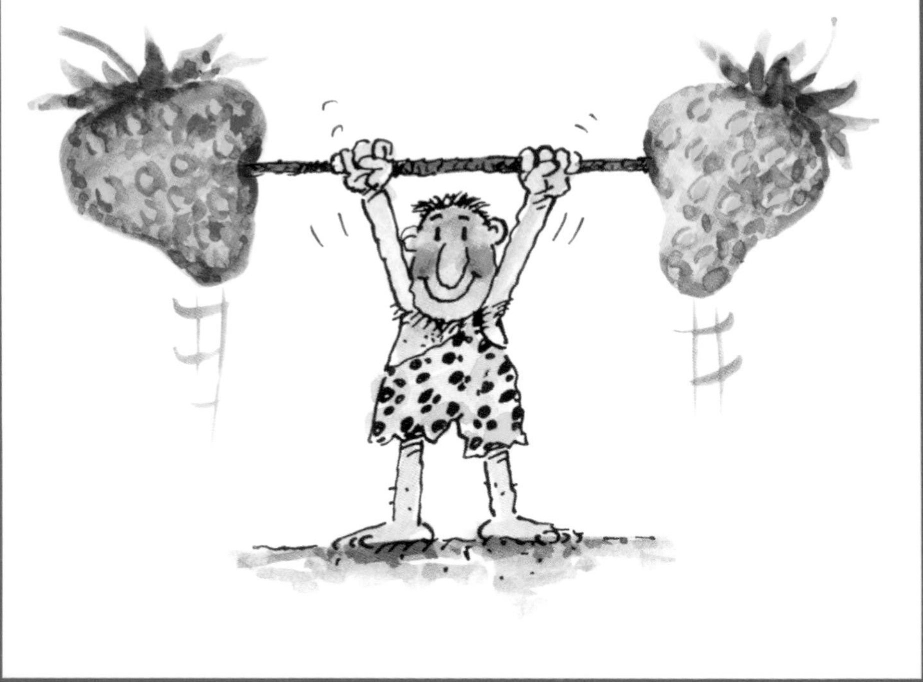

strawberry lift

toasty

plum
pudding

White Wines

Today the choices are extensive and offer many blends and alternative European varieties. The traditional Riesling and Chardonnay have been joined by wonderful Sauvignon Blanc, Semillon, Burgundy, Voignier, Pinot Gris and the list continues to grow as the smaller vineyards search for new niche markets with alternative varieties. White wines tend towards fruit flavours that are citrus, apple, pear, apricot, lychee and gooseberry with occasional vegetable flavours such as asparagus, capsicum and herbaceous tones.

The whites are generally food friendly and "safe" if unsure of which wine to order. The trends in popular varietals continue to shift and change. Whites are easy on the palate and wonderful to drink alone or with food.

They tend to be fresh, aromatic, easy to please and adapt well to many different flavours.

I cook with wine;
sometimes I even add it to the food

W.C. FIELDS

buttery

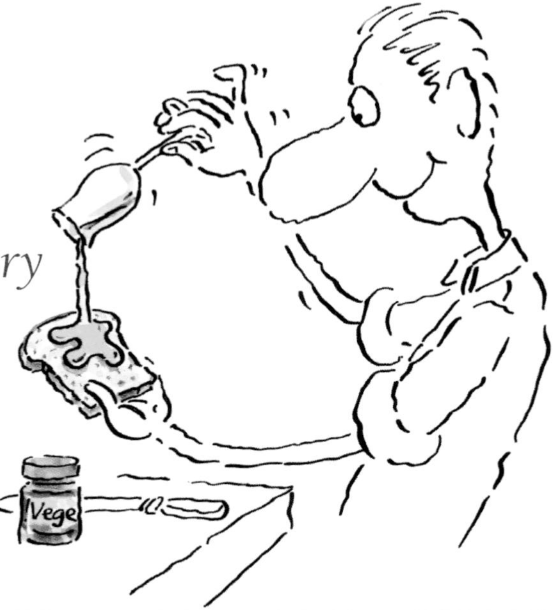
Vege

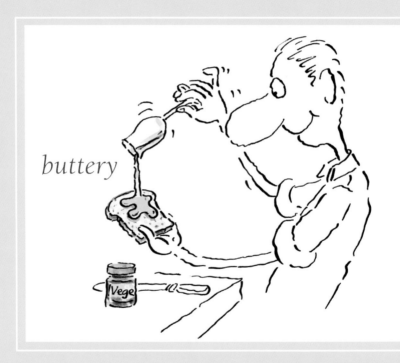

dusty

*shows
bubblegum*

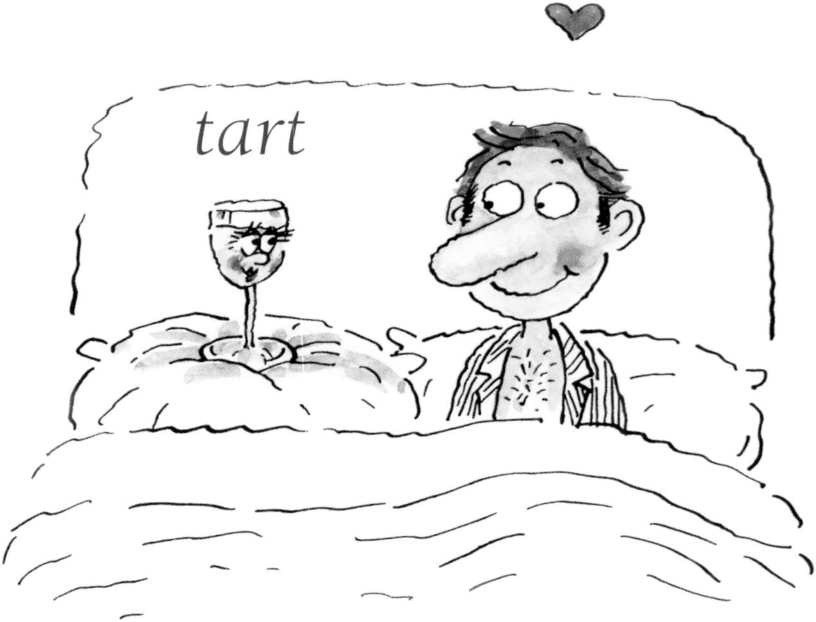
tart

slightly exotic nose

herbaceous

harmony

sweet floral nose

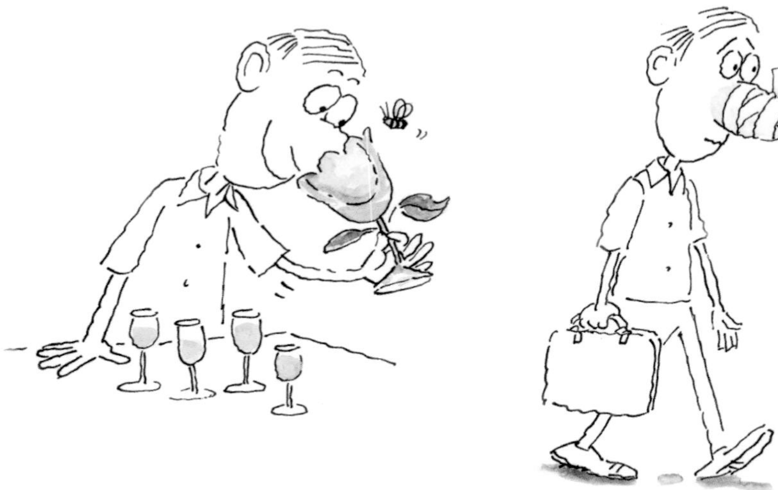

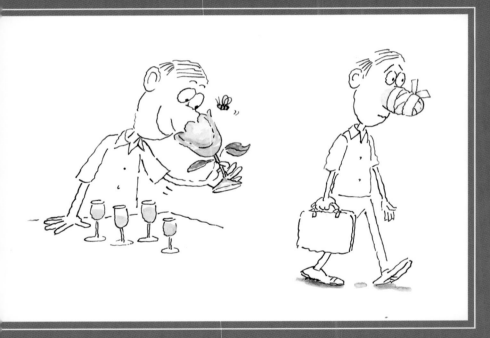

We match the style to go with the meal
This one's a good choice I feel
The promise of aromas and tastes
And a night of merriment with my mates

With anticipation we pull the cork
And there ensues much wine talk
The aromas delight and the promise of more
Leads us to indulge and make our heads sore

JUDY VALON

minty freshness

fig

charred

dry finish

"Wine is the most civilized thing
in the world."

ERNEST HEMINGWAY

gooseberry

freshly cut grass

floral
bouquet

If your heart is warm with happiness, you'll need a glass - if sorrow chills your heart, have two

LEHMUSVUORI HANNU

What though youth gave love and roses, age still leaves us friends and wine

THOMAS MOORE

Wine is bottled poetry.

ROBERT LOUIS STEVENSON

oozing apricot

Red Wines

Reds have been described as more suited to the mature palate; I understand this to mean more wine drinking experience rather than the drinker's years!

Reds can vary from the lighter styles often best served chilled through to the seriously full bodied aged varieties with muscle. These need more care and attention when storing but can be exceptionally rewarding. Mostly they are served at room temperature and if allowed to breathe a little, they will delight. From a lighter style Pinot Noir and the lesser known Nebbiolo, through to Merlot, Cabernet Sauvignon, Cabernet Franc, Grenache and Shiraz. Best served with food, whether an informal barbeque or formal dinner party, they partner well with everything from sausages to casseroles and the family roast, and are good companions to hard cheeses.

The flavours in red wines are more intense as are the tannins which can cause allergic reactions to a few of us. The flavours and aromas you will experience are notably red soft fruits, cherry, plum, blackcurrant, blackberry, strawberry and raspberry and sometimes with chocolate and tobacco tones.

Red wines are reportedly very good for us – so go on open one!

Wine improves with age- I like it the older I get

UNKNOWN

a complex little red

tannin

coffee

rich and concentrated

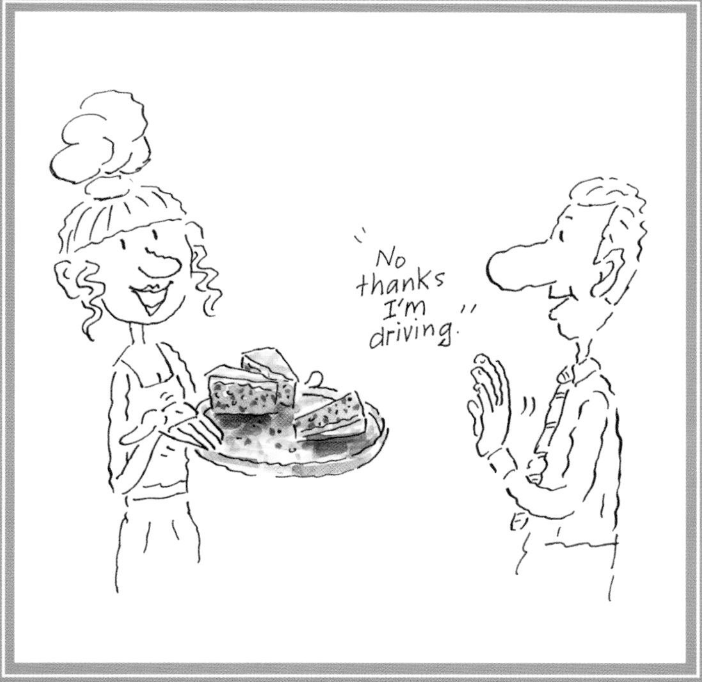
"No thanks I'm driving."

fruit cake

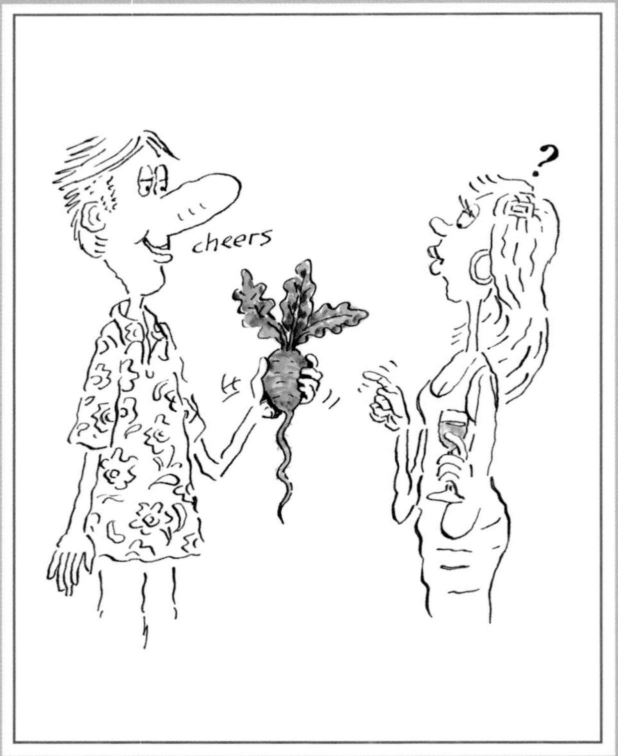
cheers
?

beetroot

*Quickly, bring me a beaker of wine,
so that I may wet my mind and say
something clever.*

ARISTOPHANES

well developed

79

brooding intensity

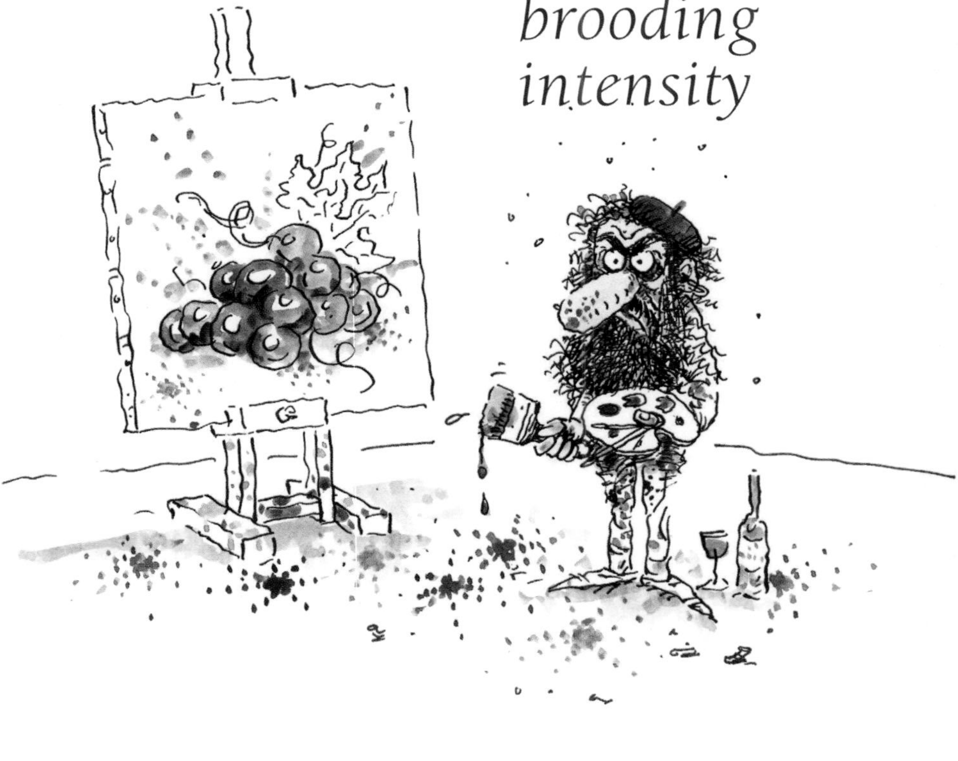

intense currant

flabby

a hint of sweaty saddle

cigar box overtones

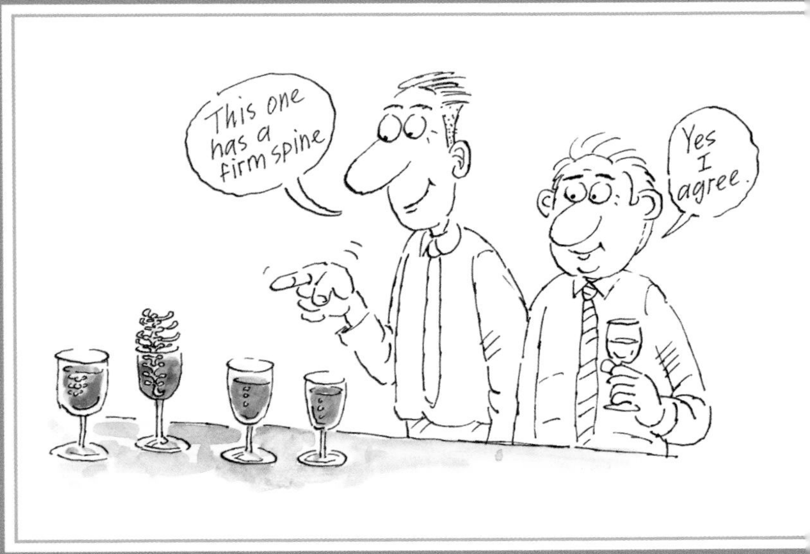
This one has a firm spine
Yes I agree.

firm structure

meaty

leathery brute

Fortified Wines

The golden and honeyed dessert wines are created by having been affected on the vine by a mould known as Noble Rot or Botrytis. This mould shrivels the grape and intensifies the sugars. Served well chilled, these are a perfectly delicious end to a meal accompanied by fruit desserts or soft cheeses. These wines will age well for several years if you can leave them alone!
Late picked varieties (Spatlese) can also be served in a similar way but are not as intensely concentrated.

A little sherry for Madame?

Long considered to be the tipple of choice for the let us say more mature of us, this however is no longer the case. They are the perfect aperitif and were originally produced in warmer regions to withstand travel. Invented by the Spanish they are the perfect companions to Tapas and nibbles. Sherry is often misunderstood, unappreciated or has been forgotten entirely. The market has been flooded by sweet sickly imitations which bear no resemblance to a refined and beautiful sherry. True Sherries take years to produce and take their complexity from ageing and blending. They should be served well chilled and are the perfect appetite wetters. Two basic styles of sherry are Fino and Amontillado.

The Australian's have a reputation of producing quality Sherries, however if you are lucky enough to be in Spain, make sure you imbibe – you will find a new appreciation of this wonderful aperitif. Just remember the alcohol content is high at 15 per cent or more.

*P*ort is a sweet, strong wine originating in Portugal, mostly made from red wines though a smaller amount of white port is also made from white grapes. The wine is made by the addition of brandy during fermentation. which stops the process before its completion. Port is then matured in wood before being bottled. Port starts out as a ruby and after ageing in wood for five years loses its intensity of colour to become tawny. Aged tawnies have been aged in wood for longer periods.

Port is an after dinner drink served with cheese or dessert and has traditionally been a male domain served (with cigars) after the ladies had retired to the drawing room.

There is a unique body of English ritual and etiquette surrounding the consumption of port, stemming from British naval custom. Traditionally, the wine is passed "port to port" the host will pour a glass for the person seated at their right, and then pass the bottle or decanter to the left in a clockwise direction.

It is considered poor form to ask for the decanter directly. Instead, the person seeking a refill would ask of the person who has the bottle: "do you know the bishop of Gloucester?" (or some other English town). If the person being asked does not know the ritual (and so replies in the negative), the querent will remark "He's an awfully nice fellow, but he never remembers to pass the port".

fortified

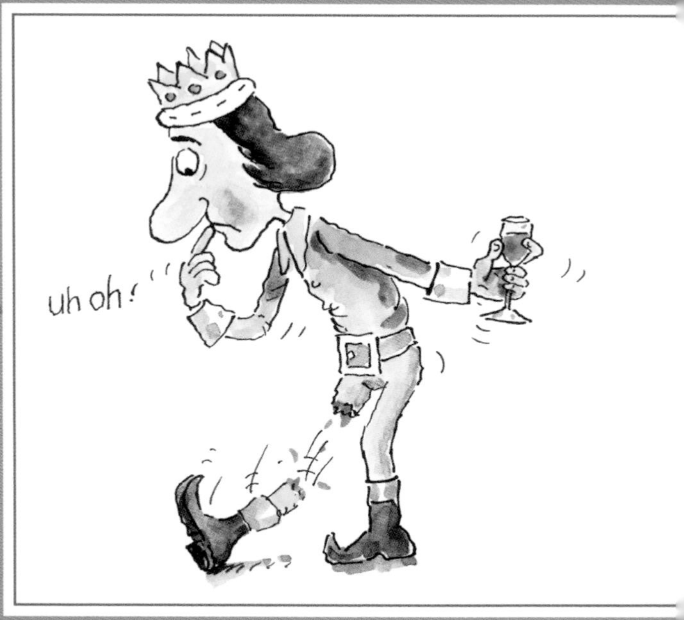
uh oh!

noble rot

Corked and Faulty Wines

Corked – with the advent of Stelvin (screw) cap and the new generation synthetic corks, this could become less common, however we may possibly encounter new problems occurring as the new closures on wines are left to age. The wine becomes tainted with mould that develops in the cork producing a damp, mouldy smell that totally dominates the bouquet of the wine.

Oxidation occurs where the wine receives too much oxygen and goes on to produce a stale smell and taste and brownish discolouration of the wine.

Volatile is when the acid (acetic acid) levels are too high and produce a wine with a pungent dominating aroma that is sharp and sour, think vinegar and nail polish remover.

corked

I have enjoyed great health at a great age,
because every day since I can remember, I have
consumed a bottle of wine except when I have not felt well.
Then I have consumed two bottles

ATTRIBUTED TO A BISHOP OF SEVILLE

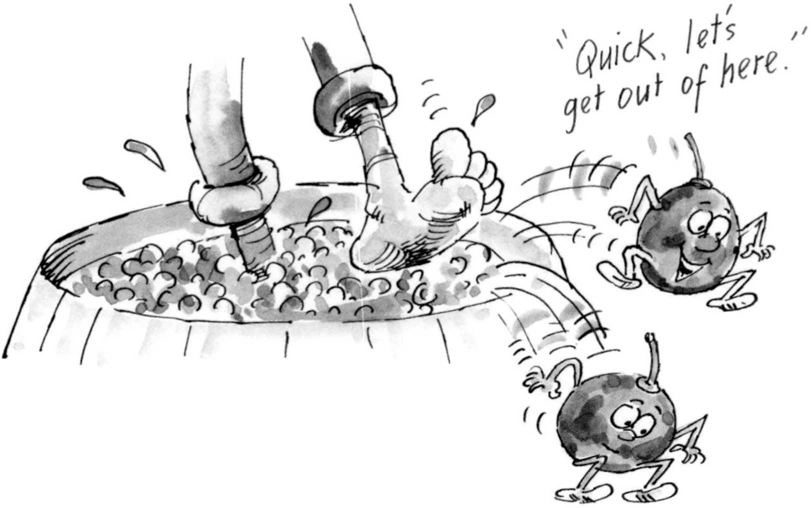
"Quick, let's get out of here."

the
grape
escape

Some of the most common tasting terms

Aromatic	Distinctive floral or herb nose. Riesling, Pinot Gris, Viognier & Sauvignon Blanc
Biscuity	Champagne methode traditionelle
Body	Texture, light, medium or full
Buttery	Champagne methode traditonelle, Chardonnay
Complex	Multi dimensional flavours (potential for ageing)
Creamy	Champagne
Crisp	Light young white wines
Dry	Wines whose final flavour in the mouth is dry
Earthy	Extra depth of fruit, Cabernet Sauvignon, Shiraz
Finish	The end flavour of the wine
Floral	Aromatic and floral. Gewurtztraminer, and Riesling
Gamey	Mature red wines, Pinot Noir, Shiraz
Herbaceous	Leafy and aromatic. Sauvignon Blanc
Leathery	Think horse saddle. Aged Pinot Noir and Shiraz
Length	The lingering aftertaste
Nutty	Aged Semillion, Chardonnay
Oaky	Matured in Oak, Chardonnay
Peppery	Spicy, freshly ground black pepper - Shiraz
Spicey	Peppery, aromatic wines. Riesling, Pinot Gris, Shiraz and Grenache
Structure	The combination of fruit, acid and tannin tastes
Tannin	Mainly in reds, the dry chalkiness
Yeasty	As for creamy, biscuity – champagne styles

*"Sometimes when I reflect back on all the wine I drink,
I feel shame. Then I look into the glass and think about the
workers in the vineyards and all of their hopes and dreams.
If I didn't drink this wine, they might be out of work
and their dreams would be shattered.*

*Then I say to myself, "It is better that I drink this wine
and let their dreams come true, rather than be selfish
and worry about my liver."*

JACK HANDY

good nose

Other Books by The Wine Appreciation Guild

"The Best Wine Publisher in the US."
—Edward Cointreau, Gourmand World Cookbook Award

A Wine Growers' Guide, Philip M. Wagner (ISBN 0-932664-92-X)
Africa Uncorked, John and Erica Platter (ISBN 1-891267-52-3)
Armagnac, Charles Neal (ISBN 1-891267-20-5)
Chow! Venice, Shannon Essa and Ruth Edenbaum (ISBN 1-934259-00-4)
Concepts in Wine Chemistry, Yair Margalit (ISBN 1-891267-74-4)
Concepts in Wine Technology, Yair Margalit (ISBN 1-891267-51-5)
Favorite Recipes of California Winemakers, (ISBN 0-932664-03-2)
Fine Wine in Food, Patricia Ballard (ISBN 0-932664-56-3)
Ghost Wineries of the Napa Valley, Irene Whitford Haynes (ISBN 0-932664-90-3)
Icon: Art of the Wine Label, JeffCaldewey and Chuck House (ISBN 1-891267-30-2)
Imagery: Art for Wine, Bob Nugent (ISBN 1-891267-30-2)
Napa Wine: A History, Charles L. Sullivan (ISBN 1-891267-07-8)
Olive Oil, Leonardo Romanelli (ISBN 1-891267-55-8)
Portugal's Wines and Wine Makers, New Ed., Richard Mason (ISBN 1-891267-01-9)
Prosciutto, Carla Bardi (ISBN 1-891267-54-X)
Red & White, Max Allen (ISBN 1-891267-37-X)
Rum, Dave Blume (ISBN 1-891267-62-0)
Tasting & Grading Wine, Clive Michelsen (9197532606)
Terroir, James E. Wilson (ISBN 1-891267-22-1)
The Bartender's Black Book, Stephen Cunningham (ISBN 1-891267-31-0)
The Champagne Cookbook, Malcolm R. Herbert (ISBN 1-891267-70-1)
The Commonsense Book of Wine, Leon D. Adams (ISBN 0-932664-76-8)
The French Paradox, Gene Ford (ISBN 0-932664-81-4)
The Global Encyclopedia of Wine, Edited by Peter Forrestal (ISBN 1-891267-38-8)
The Science of Healthy Drinking, Gene Ford (ISBN 1-891267-47-7)
The Taste of Wine, Emile Peynaud (ISBN 0-932664-64-4)
The University Wine Course, Marian Baldy (ISBN 0-932664-69-5)
The Wines of Baja California, Ralph Amey (ISBN 1-891267-65-5)
The Wines of France, Clive Coates (ISBN 1-891267-14-0)
Understanding Wine Technology, David Bird (ISBN 1-891267-91-4)
Wine Heritage, Dick Rosano (ISBN 1-891267-13-2)
Wine in Everyday Cooking, Patricia Ballard ((ISBN 0-932664-45-8)
Wine Investment for Portfolio Diversification, Mahesh Kumar (ISBN 1-891267-84-1)
Wine Lovers Cookbook, Malcolm R. Herbert (ISBN 0-932664-82-2)
Wine Marketing and Sales, Paul Wagner, Janeen Olsen & Liz Thatch (1-891267-99-X)
Winery Technology & Operations, Yair Margalit (0-932664-66-0)
World Encyclopedia of Champagne and Sparkling Wine, Tom Stevenson (1-891267-61-2)
You're a Real Wine Lover When..., Bert Witt (1-891267-25-6)
Zinfandel, Cathleen Francisco (1-891267-15-9)